COLD

COMFORT

COLD COMFORT

MAGGIE ANDERSON

For Carol, whose good words, good
friendship, and comfort are like light
and air here in Ohio, a gray place
with beautiful sunsets.

Maggie

7.11.94

UNIVERSITY OF PITTSBURGH PRESS

Published by the University of Pittsburgh Press, Pittsburgh, Pa. 15260
Copyright © 1986, Maggie Anderson
All rights reserved
Feffer and Simons, Inc., London
Manufactured in the United States of America
Second printing 1988

Library of Congress Cataloging in Publication Data

Anderson, Maggie.
    Cold comfort.

    (Pitt poetry series)
    I. Title. II. Series.
PS3551.N3745C6   1986   811'.54   86-7004
ISBN 0-8229-3542-2
ISBN 0-8229-5384-6 (pbk.)

Some of these poems have originally appeared in the following publications:
The American Poetry Review ("Civilization," "Far," "Palimpsest," and "To
Carry All of Us"); *The Missouri Review* ("The Artist"); *Northwest Review*
("Among Elms and Maples, Morgantown, West Virginia, August, 1935,"
"House and Graveyard, Rowlesburg, West Virginia, 1935," "In Singing
Weather," "Independence Day, Terra Alta, West Virginia, 1935," and "Min-
ing Camp Residents, West Virginia, July, 1935"); *The Pennsylvania Review*
("Before Winter"); *Prairie Schooner* ("Country Wisdoms" and "With Wine");
Quarterly West ("As Close"). "Related to the Sky" and "Spitting in the
Leaves" originally appeared in *Poetry East*, No. 12.
    "As Close" also appeared in the *1984 Anthology of Magazine Verse and
Yearbook of American Poetry* (Beverly Hills: Monitor Book Company, 1984).
    I would like to express my appreciation to the National Endowment for the
Arts, the Pennsylvania Council on the Arts, and the MacDowell Colony, Inc.,
for fellowships which assisted me in writing these poems.
    I would also like to thank Patricia Dobler, Lynn Emanuel, Marc Harshman,
Irene McKinney, and Maxine Scates for helpful comments on these poems;
and Elizabeth, Tom, and Anna French; Ann, Paul, and Helen Krier; Sheila
and Bob Ritzmann; and Judith Stitzel, for the grace of companionship and
dailiness.

*The publication of this book is supported by grants
from the National Endowment for the Arts
in Washington, D.C., a Federal agency,
and the Pennsylvania Council on the Arts.*

For Anna and Elizabeth

Also by Maggie Anderson:

Years That Answer
The Great Horned Owl

CONTENTS

CONTENTS

To Carry All of Us

COUNTRY WISDOMS

"Rescue the drowning and tie your shoe-strings."
—Thoreau, *Walden*

Out here where the crows turn around
where the ground muds over and the snow fences bend
we've been bearing up. Although

a green winter means a green graveyard
and we've buried someone every month since autumn
warm weather pulls us into summer by the thumbnails.

They say these things.

When the April rains hurl ice chunks onto the banks
the river later rises to retrieve them.
They tell how the fierce wind from the South

blows branches down, power lines and houses
but always brings the trees to bud.
Fog in January, frost in May

threads of cloud, they say, rain needles.
My mother would urge, be careful what you want,
you will surely get it.

More ways than one to skin that cat.
Then they say, Boot straps.
Pull yourself up.

PALIMPSEST

1.

Mornings, the sun catches the slant of the slate roof
and the flanks of the young workhorses as they walk
the training ring with their black blinders in place.
The ring is a perfect circle of light. The horses
do not know how far they have to go before they can stop.
They do not know that they are going nowhere.
They do not know how their bodies take them there
but they do. The horses hear the whip and feel the blinders.
The dust spreads. Everything the horses leave behind,
the tracks they cover and recover, the white circle,
the morning light, palimpsest.

2.

What if you were to live somewhere far from here?
Somewhere, perhaps, like Alliance, Ohio, where
you would lay your whole life down on the brick streets
under the big maples with their yellow leaves in autumn?
Somewhere where you would suddenly remember how blue
the sky opens out, how the cornstalks shamble for miles,
how the highway's straight all the way to Wyoming?
You might live there for years and talk only with friends.
You might die there and be buried on the only hill around,
the hill that stands above the field of pumpkins in October
like the protector of orange. You might become
the protector of orange, having nothing to do
but watch the light shift in the sky, the fields
as they rustle and fade away, the pumpkins
as they dissolve in their skins, holding in
moisture like extravagant kisses
until the last possible moment.

3.

Now there are no people on this beach, only waves
and bathhouses and shiny grains of sand.
Inside the little rooms the bathers are assembling
their clothing, layer by layer, to face the gray sea.
Inside it smells of salt and wet wood. The bathers
pocket their wristwatches and rings and count their change.
                              When they open the doors,
the sudden wind will slap against their unaccustomed
skins and make the waves sound more violent
than they are on this quiet strip of beach.
Some bathers will test the water first
with their feet, at the white edge. Others
will kneel in the sand and wet their hands
splattering the air with stones and kelp.
Most of them will leap quickly out past the breakers
to where the sand will be softer and the water more calm.
                              The bathers
in the wooden sheds are thinking just how deep
toward the distance they will dare to go.
They are wondering if it will be as far
as they had wanted to go before they opened
the thin doors to the water, before they spotted
the tiny white boats at the horizon.

RELATED TO THE SKY

At dusk, the blue line of these hills looks,
of course, like waves. So I wave. Hello hills.
Being hills, they do not speak back but just
draw in more light. Clouds, a small platoon
of healing hands, brush the trees. I try to find
the exact spot of the stars I liked in last night's
sky. Impossible. The leaves sift and muffle,
make room for the moon. I try to remember the color
of those leaves, how they were. Their shaggy
shapes, now draped in dark, cover the round animal
back of the hills. I try to remember how it was
once ocean floor and will be again, ancestral
and related to the sky.

CEMETERY,
SAINT JOSEPH'S SETTLEMENT

Having slept here and awakened among tombstones
and yellow fields, I feel affection for the Germans
who found this place over a century ago and stopped,
preferring to look down on the Ohio River forever
than to cross it. Some of them were born in German
and died in English: *geboren* 1848, died 1869
and none of them lived long. I walk past faded
granite Stations of the Cross and think of those
who've stayed, the descendants who live here now
in clean white houses. My connection to these people,
having slept an afternoon in full sun among their dead,
seems as deep as my connection to you after ten years.
I know the concealed bones of these Germans now
as I know your back in sleep, and this lush grass feels
familiar as your hair. This is the intimacy history
allows: to find a beautiful place and to remain there.
This is the embrace of ambiguity that says, as these
people must have to each other before they fixed
the rafters for the barns, Yes, that's the Ohio
and beyond it, the West, but here, we choose
to stop and make our settlement. Here, we will
build our houses, care for the children, educate
ourselves and bury what dies, among us.

WITH WINE

Es war nicht in mir. Es ging aus und ein.
Da wollt ich es halten. Da hielt es der Wein.
　　　　—Rilke, "Das Lied Des Trinkers"

Now it is October, after harvest, and the fields fill up
with leaves and heavy rain. Someone has left our company
tonight and gone out to the dark pine forest where she
will drink alone in the rain. I do not want to laugh
at her as some do, speculating indiscreetly around
the dinner table, nor will I go out after her tonight
as the kind man putting on his jacket says he wants to.

I have been out there so many times myself,
because something frightened me in what passed by
as witty talk, because I heard again the imaginary
friends, calling from my childhood in the voices
no one ever could believe, calling with cold comfort
in the wine. Or I have gone because I know it is a time
of war, or nearly war, and there is nothing I can do.

I have run, as she will, from those who called me
to come back. I have staggered out to sit alone
on mossy rocks with wine and study the divisions
in branches of the trees, too sensible they seemed
to me, uninteresting, like pleats I hadn't planned on
in the sky, even though I might invent them into stars.

It is always nearly time of war. Tonight, because
I know she's out there, I don't have to be. She does
our work alone as I sit warm and calm beside the fire,
certain she is busy, following the blur of pines
out into the fields, tracking down our burdens:
everything that holds us and what we lose with wine,
what we think we have to gather in all by ourselves.

THE WASH IN MY
GRANDMOTHER'S ARMS

In the only photograph of my paternal grandmother
she wears an apron and a dust cap, holds
her washing in her arms, and squints at the camera
as if she finds photography too theoretical,
its attempt to capture history as it's made.
I never knew my grandmother but I've heard stories:
how she never wanted anyone to marry, how she feared
thunderstorms and the whistles as helper trains
pushed forty times their weight up Laurel Mountain.
My grandmother had seven children, no teeth,
and no belief in medicine. I recognize my relative
by her suspicion of impropriety in taking pictures.

It's my grandmother's conviction that, like lightning
or heavy trains on mountain sides working against
gravity, photography and marriage leave too much
to chance, to interpretation later of expression
or disaster. She is clearly overworked and resists
this fixing of the present in a beautiful nostalgia,
the diurnal translated as the representative.
My grandmother clutches her wash in the wind
and I locate my inheritance: how she holds to her task
in the face of speculation, as if the picture could
not possibly turn out, as if the sheets were trying
to fly away from her like pale extinct birds.

GRAY

Driving through the Monongahela Valley in winter
is like driving through the gray matter
of someone not too bright but conscientious,
a hard-working undergraduate who barely passes.
Everybody knows how hard he tries. I'm driving up
into gray mountains and there, it may be snowing
gray, little flecks like pigeon feathers, or what
used to sift down onto the now abandoned slag piles,
like what seems to sift across the faces
of the jobless in the gray afternoons.

At Johnstown I stop, look down the straight line
of the Incline, closed for repairs, to the gray heart
of the steel mills with For Sale signs on them. Behind me,
is the last street of disease-free Dutch elms in America,
below me, a city rebuilt three times after flood.
Gray is a lesson in the poise of affliction. Disaster
by disaster, we learn insouciance, begin to wear
colors bright as the red and yellow sashes on
elephants, whose gray hides cover, like this sky,
an enormity none of us can fathom, though we try.

TO CARRY ALL OF US

Only responsible people keep cows. If you buy near cattle,
you can count on your neighbors to be home repairing fences.
Cows don't know how much they cost, or yield, and cats
are free. I always cried, as a child, when we drove
past the stockyard and had to hear the cattle, moaning
because crowded, not knowing they were going to die.
It's still their ignorance that breaks my heart.

How elaborately the savings of the desperate poor pile up:
old car parts and empty bottles, broken dolls and rusty
buckets hung on nails, and always cats, who seek the indigent
out. As a child, I preferred the littered farms,
where, it seemed to me, the accumulation
was, like art, arranged by some design.

And as a child, I'd be horse to my friend Patty
with her brace and orthopedic shoe. A rope around my waist,
I'd gallop easy so Patty could keep up and we'd run
to the hilltop to see all the farms. Once, a bearded woman
in overalls and army jacket, screamed at us to get away
from her collected bounty spreading out from the porch
to her unposted fields. She spooked the cattle
next farm over, and they took off so their hooves
shook the ground where we stood. I took off too
and Patty tugged my rope, but I was wild enough
to carry her despite her limp. I was wild and strong enough
to carry all of us. I could be a bearded woman on a porch
and still have cows and not care how I dressed. I could
yell at little girls who pretended to be horses, save
everything that ever came to me: all my cats lined up
on tidy fences, my cattle never slaughtered for money.

11

WHAT I'M LEARNING FROM
YOUR CHILDHOOD

Sometimes in sleep you frown, as if dreaming
you're a child again in Denmark in the war,
your mother standing by your father
in his dress blues at the window, their eyes
fixed on German planes humming down over
red tile roofs and copper steeples.

In the Resistance, your parents made
your legacy: subversion, the simple cold
shoulder to threats on life or principle.
When we argue, I always want you to speak up.
You insist it's so American, all this fuss
and display, this announcement of intention.

When you dream the war, you dream
the bag of clothes and toys your mother
sent you off with and you wake frightened
in your native tongue because your older brother
kicked a German—*Jens har sparket en Tysker!*—
and he will die for his bravado.

From your bad dream, I am learning,
past my American trust in debate,
how sometimes a busy quiet is the only
good defense. Now, I frown too in sleep.
In my dream, I'm planting dogwood trees
to bring back balance to the air.

And it works. The sun returns. I tamp down
the roots without a word, as determined as a Dane
the morning the Germans set their bombs to Tivoli,
their boots to the cobbled streets of København,
and discovered all the Danish children sent away
and no one talking, and no Jews to be found.

Belongings

AS CLOSE

I could stay awake for years driving the nighttime
streets of this West Virginia city in a rusted VW
that doesn't belong to me. I am alive in October, ready
to record the rise in the wind. It's because of the leaves.
How they shine from the inside with that bright light.
How they shift their colors from hour to hour, how they
traipse around the bends of the Kanawha like scrip
pulsing down to the coal towns. I don't want anyone
I've ever loved to leave me now. I want all my friends
and old lovers and the children I know to stand beside me
and push their heels with mine down into the damp ground
if it rains. I want us all to stand together in our red boots
in the early morning fog, watching the wet webs on the weeds
and connecting our strong eyes to their fragility.
If we begin to cry, I want us to know it's because of the way
our shirt sleeves brush against our own arms and each other's,
as close as the coming snow will be to the stark trees
and the black branches it will pack up into.

SPITTING IN THE LEAVES

In Spanishburg there are boys in tight jeans,
mud on their cowboy boots and they wear huge hats
with feathers, skunk feathers they tell me.
They do not want to be in school, but are.
Some teacher cared enough to hold them. Unlike
their thin disheveled cousins, the boys on Matoaka's
Main Street in October who loll against parking meters
and spit into the leaves. Because of them, someone
will think we need a war, will think the best solution
would be for them to take their hats and feathers,
their good country manners and drag them off somewhere,
to Vietnam, to El Salvador. And they'll go.
They'll go from West Virginia, from hills and back roads
that twist like politics through trees, and they'll fight,
not because they know what for but because what they know
is how to fight. What they know is feathers,
their strong skinny arms, their spitting
in the leaves.

THE CHOICES OF HORSES

I slow the car beside two horses,
motionless and bent to graze
in October twilight. They stand
in purple shadow and I can't tell
which is older. Their red manes
and their flanks pick up and warm
the yellow sun to copper.

Choice is, among other things, like this:
clear, as I pretend the choices
of these horses are, and difficult.
They could stand like this forever,
allowing dark to cover them until
the sun would rise and reveal them again
in morning frost. But they'd never know
just why they stayed. They could move off
into the forest, become a wedge of night
beyond the fields. But they'd never reassemble
just that pose they're holding now,
that grace of companionship and dailiness.

When I round the curve, the line of sun is gone.
I can't locate the horses in this light.
They've dissolved into their choices
as I named them: poised where they were,
or galloping off among the trees.
I only hear them now, or imagine that I do,
whinnying through the grasses in the night.

BELONGINGS

Things stay on in the world past value.
We cannot hold them, cannot give them up.
My fingers falter on frayed lace and I want
to turn from its survival, all the work
it takes to make a pretty thing last.
I stay away from second-hand stores:
the rows of shoes children have outgrown,
shirts the dead leave to be washed,
or what I imagine is some man's only
necktie, draped over a broken game.

The pewter napkin rings and boxes full
of fine bone china from my father endure
past my sentiment or shame. I keep them
still, though locked away, like the memory
of blue taffeta my mother wore, before,
near death, she turned her face from all
the weather. I can't stand old work clothes
hung in chifforobes, the cloying smells
of musk and oleander, can't bear to touch
belongings no one wants any longer.

INDEPENDENCE DAY
TERRA ALTA, WEST VIRGINIA, 1935

Maple trees rise around the picnic tables
as if an extension of the crowd. The young man
in the white linen suit and cap imagines himself
more dapper, and the girls selling kisses
under the striped canopy bend their heads.
Another girl, in a middy blouse with a party hat
tilted on her head, snarls at Walker Evans.
She doesn't want her picture made beside her mother
who is wearing a cloth coat with a fur collar
in early July, with the heat washing the fairgrounds
and everyone she knows standing around. She knows
what Evans doesn't: the talk behind the chance booth,
the way every gesture falls on her in a long shadow
of judgment and kin, her small mother in her stupid
cloth coat, clutching her purse to her bosom.

AMONG ELMS AND MAPLES
MORGANTOWN, WEST VIRGINIA,
AUGUST, 1935

Houses are wedged between the tall stacks
of Seneca Glass beside the Monongahela
and waffle up steep hills. Here, the terrain
allows photographers to appear acrobatic.
Walker Evans liked standing on a hill, focusing
down so it seemed he was poised on a branch.
He liked the single telephone pole against
the flat sky, crossed off-center like a crucifix.
Beneath it, among elms and maples, is the house
my mother lived in with her sister and their mother
nearly fifty years ago. In this shot, Evans
only wanted the rough surfaces of clapboard
houses, their meshed roofs and slanted gables.
He didn't want my mother peeling the thin skin
from tomatoes with a sharp knife, my clumsy
Aunt Grace chasing the ones she'd dropped
around the linoleum floor. That would be another
picture, not this one. I look back from the future,
past the undulating, unremitting line of hills
Evans framed my family in, through the shaggy fronds
of summer ferns he used as foreground and as border.

MINING CAMP RESIDENTS
WEST VIRGINIA, JULY, 1935

They had to seize something in the face of the camera.
The woman's hand touches her throat as if feeling
for a necklace that isn't there. The man buries one hand
in his overall pocket, loops the other through a strap,
and the child twirls a strand of her hair as she hunkers
in the dirt at their feet. Maybe Evans asked them to stand
in that little group in the doorway, a perfect triangle
of people in the morning sun. Perhaps he asked them
to hold their arms that way, or bend their heads. It was
his composition after all. And they did what he said.

STREET SCENE
MORGANTOWN, WEST VIRGINIA, 1935

Neither of the black women behind the table
confronts the camera. I know this street,
High Street in Morgantown, where Walker Evans
documents the resourcefulness of poverty,
its make-do and carry-on by calculating
what to sell, or raise to sell, or what
to barter when all the cash is gone.
The women's dark faces are exhausted
from such improvisation. They look away,
will not look a white man,
even with a camera, in the eyes.

They have to think of everything: how long
before food spoils in the heat, how much money
a cake's worth, how cautious their conversation
has to be with customers. My mother might have
bought from them. I wish I knew if she was polite,
if she could afford to be. I wonder how aware
she might have been of the men, who loiter
across the street in straw hats, smoking cigars,
reflected in the plate glass window above
the table so they rise like ghosts of abstract
thought behind the women's turned heads.

HOUSE AND GRAVEYARD
ROWLESBURG, WEST VIRGINIA, 1935

I can't look long at this picture, a Walker Evans photograph
of a West Virginia graveyard in the Great Depression,
interesting for the sharp light it throws
on poverty, intimate for me because it focuses
on my private and familial dead. This is where

my grandparents, my Uncle Adrian and my Aunt Margaret
I am named for are buried. Adrian died at seven, long
before I was born. Margaret died in childbirth in 1929.
The morning sun falls flat against the tombstones
then spreads across Cannon Hill behind them. I see

how beautiful this is even though everyone was poor,
but in Rowlesburg nothing's changed. Everything
is still the same, just grayer. Beside the graveyard
is Fike's house with the rusty bucket, the tattered
trellis and the same rocker Evans liked. Miss Funk,

the school teacher, now retired, and her widowed sister
still live down the road out of the camera's range.
I remember how my Aunt Nita loved that mountain,
how my father told of swinging from the railroad
bridge down into the Cheat. Nita worked

for the Farm Security Administration too, as Evans did.
She checked people's houses for canned goods, to see
how many they had stored, and she walked the road
by here, every day. I can't look long at this picture.
It warps my history into politics, makes art

of my biography through someone else's eyes.
It's a good photograph, but Walker Evans
didn't know my family, nor the distance
his careful composition makes me feel now
from my silent people in their graves.

Dream Vegetables

THE ARTIST

Tamsen Donner, laying out her linens
in Illinois and packing up the books
for the school she would start in California,
had no way of knowing if any of the children
playing in the red dust by the wagons might
be an artist. But eight-year-old Patty Reed
sitting on the wagon tongue talking
to her doll, knew even then what would be
required of her on the trail. She knew
it would be her own flat insistence
and determination—"God has not
brought us this far to let us perish
now"—that would keep the armed men
of the Relief Party to the task of bearing
famished children on their backs through
waist-deep snow. Patty Reed knew
to pack up a satchel to carry out with her,
as she'd seen her mother and Tamsen Donner
do, before they left the States. She knew
enough to hide it from the practical men,
risking their lives to take her down
the mountains. She carried it with her,
underneath her clothing, through the High
Sierra snows, away from the yellow light
of the fire at Alder Creek, where the dried
flesh she had eaten was the mule she had ridden
through the Wasatch. She carried out three things:
a small glass saltcellar, her black-eyed doll,
a lock of her dead grandmother's hair.
When Patty Reed was safe at last in the warm
camp in the foothills, she lifted up her thin

dress and unwrapped her little bundle. The men
moved away from her and said nothing, as,
past her hunger, she brought out these things
of beauty and of memory, and began to play.

TO DRAW PICTURES

Draw what you see just how you see it,
strings of trees or hills with faces. So much
depends on where you live. Name what you draw
by where it is: Utah scape, or Texas scape,
or scape of windows and the sea. Draw
horizon right up front and put the sky
on top. Draw fast, past your vocabulary
and the hope of some eventual display.
Let the landscapes tell you what they say.
Let things have conversations and connect
them with your lines: typewriter to curtain
rod, fireplace to davenport, vegetables
to moon. Forget what you don't know, or do,
of composition. Just fill the space and use
all the colors as you guess they were.
Don't keep your pictures. Give them up
to children and their friends. For them,
put in something that does not belong.

EXPOSURE

The yellow squash sleep in skins covered by dirt
and their own extravagant leaves, large as their dreams
and as embarrassing. Because their bodies are both
crumpled and appealing, they dream of being utterly
naked on a busy street in a large city. They bend
the crooks of their necks to cover themselves and
curl up among their own stalks like shy bananas.
Suddenly they realize the crowd that has gathered,
if not applauding, is at least not throwing stones.
The pulp of the squash is as heavy as wet sand.
In full baskets, they reflect the sun.

FALLING

Lashed to stakes with scraps of old shirt
the tomatoes dream sudden descent. The need
for sleep fills them and they seem to weigh
more than they do. They jerk softly among
wet leaves into the dreams that continue the life,
its unexpected inclines and crevices, its slatternly
dirt rows. The tomatoes shake hard and awaken
to the clear and permanent sky. The next dream
is under the same sun, the same tomatoes,
ready to edge toward sleep once more, vermilion.

EXAMINATION

How clever of the peas to sleep three rows over,
nearer the light! The adolescent beans, mudded
to their trellises, know this arrangement well.
They dream of failure. The wire they suffer
themselves around is their conspicuous cheat.
They are the obese and the ridiculed, the cheaply
clothed. Even when the sun shines the beans dream
dumb, caught copying. They cower under their foliage
so no one will notice, and still they dream the test.
Their brown seeds swell, too large for consumption,
and they dream exhausted by fecundity.

NIGHTMARE

The soft moist brown decay beneath hard leaves
makes cabbages sometimes have awful dreams.
They know the source, in need, the ache that cleaves
them from companions, but cannot grasp the means
of changing what they fear. They sleep alone.
In dream, the cabbages are haunted, tracked
through winding passages where they can't run,
straight into culverts where they can't turn back.
They dream the shaggy roots of those they've loved
but never have come through for. Too much head!
They do not use it wisely. High above
the warm sun burns their rounded husks to red.
The cabbages dream all they did not seize,
when they were young in limp, ungoverned leaves.

INSOMNIA

The radishes pace in their red plaid bathrobes
and wish for sleep. They grow up and down
simultaneously and are preoccupied. Their green
tops keep them awake like fast conversation
they feel compelled to be in on, while
the white tangled threads of their pale roots
drag them down. They should have said something
else. They flush and fidget in the light topsoil
like reprimanded pups. Radishes sear the tongue,
the aftertaste of vigilance. They dream the burning
need for dream, the black dirt that won't go away,
the fear of intimacy, of breathing.

RECURRING

The potatoes dream black smell of water deep
underground. They hold each other by ragged
strings and swish green headdresses in small
pools of mud. Potatoes dream their own
genetics, the predictable gossip of growth.
And they keep on dreaming it: the useless
berries their leaves invent, the digging out,
the clean uplifting, then the root cellar, one
slice saved to plant again in freezing ground.

FLYING

The corn is the enormous yellow dirigible
of the August fields and it dreams fair
weather. Its husk is its own green life
raft, sliding past clouds and irrelevant
gravity. The largest phenomenon of food
in dream, corn hugs the air, dives and
pirouettes, slick as melted butter, silk
tassels flattened back, wind in the ears.

NAP DREAMS

Tarragon, basil, parsley, dill, the noisy smells
at the front of the garden by the marigolds never
sleep long. Their dreams are only a brief reprieve
from aroma. They drowse among the warm bees
and grow into condiments. The purple basil
has tiny sauce dreams; the tarragon dreams
chicken. The parsley dreams potato's little
sister, the pillowslip's green crewel. The dill
hovers over all the rows and drifts yellow seeds
onto cucumbers it schemes to marry, to gain
citizenship in the alien country of solid food.
Rarely do the herbs remember their dreams, their
swift, upright lapses of industry.

SWEET RESIN

This is my nap among the pines: four o'clock
in the afternoon, I've had a bath and am drying
in warm air, sleepy on the high bed in the room
with twelve windows. When I close my eyes,
a dark green scurry of piano music crosses
the blue field I try to keep uncluttered
in my mind. I listen for the regular ticking
of cicadas in the meadow grass, smell the onions
and red peppers cooking downstairs in garlic
butter and basil, the smell of being cared for.
Further back in the woods, a screen door closes,
the sound carries, and the pine trees ease themselves
into my room, brushing past the chairs and dresser
to lie down with me. Their wide boughs are blanket
enough for the breeze, and their long needles,
soft as scarf fringe, make wet tracks
of sweet resin on my wrists and thighs.

ART IN AMERICA

Three of us, two poets and one painter,
drive out into clear autumn weather
to gather in some harvest
from the roadside stands
where pumpkins are piled up
like huge orange marbles in the sun
and the gray Hubbard squash
are disguised as blue toy tops among
blueberries and jugs of apple cider.
We have to make our choices,
as in art, calculate the risk
of making them too ordinary, pale,
like a pool ball hit too thin
because we get afraid
when the table's so alive.
We also risk bravado
(too many pumpkins, or too large)
and, since nothing's ever free,
we might have to put things back.
But today, we think we'll
get it right because
we're not alone
and we're laughing,
arguing a bit,
examining the vegetables,
making up our minds, and
saying how we think we might
believe in the perfection
of communities of artists,
the common work among us.
What one of us does not get said,
the others will.

In Singing Weather

"Nature is a Haunted House—but Art—a House that tries to be haunted."

—Emily Dickinson, letter to Thomas Wentworth Higginson, 1876

1.

In September, third quarter moon
andante over first frost and that screech owl
is back again all night in the woods
below my house. Stray weeds
shift, directionless,
left too long alone.

Something's too rigid in this weather
as if it doesn't believe in itself
like the posturings of my own mind at twenty,
rushing at the delicacy I would have embraced.
And yet each thing connects to every other,

especially in memory we rely on these links,
contrapuntal: the hinge on the high school door
connects to my red hat, or to the warm brass
bracelets wrapping an arm I once caressed.
My dead parents, standing hand in hand
on a trellised porch, come back

with the evening sun. The September breeze
is a mannered piano, holding nothing
full-bodied or building for storm,
only each thing poised without words
against every other, the echo
of that screech owl, back.

2.

In Indian summer we know
the cold days have been only a trick
the weather plays in early autumn.
Like the dog at the screen door
wanting in, the heat is back now
in the afternoons, the summer holding.

In my garden, the wet tomato vines
are heavy laden and persistent
as a bagpipe drone, a burden
to be dealt with. So I pick
tomatoes and preserve them. So much
to do this time of year

yet the garden manages
to bear fruit as it decays
and the music of this weather
is as resonant as first
desire, the summer holding
just a little longer.

3.

When the wind of October rises up under doorways
lifting winter from the plains after just
one warm day in ten, it beats against my vision
of the future, another end: one more
finished summer of melted grainy afternoons.

The dogs run restless at my calling,
far to the next hilltop, awash in weather
and frenzied disobedience. Me too, if someone
would dare to call me from this wind, now pulling
rain, inexorably pulling winter.

Even a dignified music with trumpets
couldn't match this wind, and today it's not
music I want to hear but the howling, whining
through silhouetted leaves of the wind
giving song to the season, point

against point. Dogs barking from dark
line of hill and the mottled moon rising
through red and yellow leaves in early cold.
Nights like these the future takes hold, latching
onto the places we already understand it:

prescience knit to sentimentality. It's time now
to speak loudly and clearly and straight into the wind
from which the dogs at last turn back; noses to the dirt
they track my boot scent, eight quick paws crunching cornstalks,
four long ears whipping dust up into wind.

4.

The light revolves in its own whimsy
largo through branches and falling leaves:
the hard blues now of shuffle and dip,
plunked banjo, fiddle wheeze and guitar.

All through the pale October dusk I have called out,
called out but made no sound. The hills, tucked
in red blankets of sun, are my voice for this weather,
my round cousins. When I can't sing, they lull the sky

and improvise limpid tunes for the barns.
My voice makes only faint and courtly gestures
toward the rim of light, off, there, another
scene I named badly, another collapse of words.

Even the dogs won't go out in this weather.
Tonight is not a night for walking but for sitting
still on the soft warm rugs of winter coming,
hard blues, and the laying in.

5.

Perched on the kitchen table I look out
at morning fog so thick it muffles
even its own soft noise over white November
fields and does not burn off by noon

but goes on covering us all day. A year
has seemed a month or less, yet I find
I don't work harder, now I'm dying faster,
just pay more careful attention to the sky.

Nearly all the yellow leaves are gone
and those plants I hung to give green
this winter cover the whole window now
greener every day against white mist.

Fuga, from the Latin, *flight,* and in the long
rests I think I hear *glissando,* egregious
narrowing down to that raw muscle,
my heart, with its hum of longing.

Still, I am less grim in fog and bare trees
than in October with that crazy wind. Grandeur
makes me nervous, and now the ravaged ground
and shabby bean vines seem, at least, to match

my soul. Where there is congruence, there is
hope. After long silence, there might be music,
subtle and insistent as the Hudson River,
tidal, as far north as Troy.

6.

At the winter solstice I know again
the only point is to catch the light,
the soft shading behind black branches
against white sky. I try to hold
this moment of change in the sun
the east lit up in negative,
the hills to the south glowing
from inside, and the dark sweep
where the leaves were carried off into clouds
or another range of hills. The point, after all,
is to say only: winter light, what's here.

The brown summer boxes of leaves thrown down
and abandoned are now resurrected in dirt,
in the vacancy under the curve of fence line,
in the deeper shadow where the road
lies hung in its ruts. I give rapt
attention to weather and record it:
the solid black trunks of the oaks,
the small evening fires.
A formal music comforts
by velocity of measure and thin melody
cello obligato, the deep soft voice of coming snow.

7.

Even the breathless dead seem,
sometimes, nevertheless, to sing.

At last it's snowed and hushed the hills,
all the forest veins revealed.

The December sky is generous once more
with a light tender as a ragtime piano

frowsy as the woman who plays it by ear
and tilts her head. She's hard as nails.

Her hands build bookcases and every ivory shelf thrums,
as she jumps all her tricky sweetness off the stool

and onto the floor. She sings in a frolic fast
as a running heart, each note wound to every other.

After long silence, there is music again,
thin lip of moon and again bright stars,

the weeds, safe now in their coffins of ice,
in singing weather. The pets of my childhood

nose the white drifts in bright collars
and bows and I whistle them home to me,

in from the cold. Now the formal dead
can love me back, with their voices

carried on the wind. And I can hold them,
rock them in my own melodic arms.

Heart Fire

SMALL CITIZENS

Today was my political nap.
I lay down to it, febrile with accumulated
rage at poverty and hunger in the world,
as if they were my own shameful secrets.
I forced my eyelids shut and behind them
could still see the red roof across the street,
shiny, and healing as valerian in sunlight.
A stone was rolling down to the tin gutter
with the thunkety assurance of my five-year-old
cries from the playground in Fort Lee
when the ice cream truck would ring its bell
and stop beside the green park bench.
We children were citizens, even then,
and our city had a chain link fence
beyond which we could just make out
the grid of windows on the brick apartments
where our mothers or housekeepers labored
and watched us from above. I couldn't
read then and thought the Newark airport
lights were Russian bombs. How could I
have known what my own mother meant
by her anger at nobody I knew? She told me,
when I asked, *Politics means money, who
has it and who doesn't.* So, for a brief time,
in the early 1950s, this was my one clear
political vision: from sandbox and swings
our high voices shouted, *ice cream,* as
warm nickels tumbled down from the hands
of women, their faces full of charity
and blessing at the opened windows.

THE ONLY JAZZ BAR IN SALT LAKE

Personal history isn't a once opulent hotel
grown seedy and boarded up for winter, though
most of our language for it is. Wouldn't it be better
to talk about our pasts the way children talk about
the dinosaurs, in esoteric language they love
for its remoteness from their lives? They learn
Latin names for lumbering extinct beasts the way
I've learned the old jazz, what a blue seventh is
and how to listen for it. They know the brontosaurus
body, free of memory's complications, as I know
Art Tatum's belly at the keyboard, or Chick Webb's
flashy hands when he played at the old Savoy.
Here, in the only jazz bar in Salt Lake,
we're leaning our heads together
in a high wooden booth while a sleepy scat
singer does an old Billie Holiday song
at a wheezy mike, and you're asking me again
if I can remember how the coal trucks cool
their brakes at the bottom of the Spall Lick Hill
back home, how ironweed and joe-pye shine across
September fields. We're talking in exaggerated
West Virginia accents, trying to keep them pure
in desert air, though we know how quickly a familiar
speech flattens into mannerism, and all the loved
particulars only make us lonely. Wouldn't it be better
just to make our conversation keep its distance?
All-we've-been-through could become just this bar,
the very way we're sitting now, the smarmy stumble
of that woman's voice. We could tell our history
like stories of the dinosaurs, intricate verbiage,
with no referents anyone has ever seen.

IN MY MOTHER'S HOUSE

In the dream she is never sick and it is
always summer. She wears a polished cotton
sundress with wide shoulder straps, sits calmly
in a wooden lawn chair, green, I remember

from a photograph. I wonder if she'll know me
now, but want to keep formality awhile. I shake
her hand and introduce her to my friends,
who seem more like my parents' friends than mine,

subdued, and gathering with wine glasses
on the grass. Then I'm in the house my mother's
lived in since her death and she has changed
her clothes, put on her plaid viyella shirt.

She's sitting in her attic, among suitcases
and webs of boxes. A yellow triangle of light
skims the floor into the lap of her wool skirt.
I have had to be resourceful to get to her,

climbing up a bright blue ladder to the window
that broke down as I came through, transformed
itself from glass back into sand. My mother
holds a glass jar in her hands. She seems

preoccupied, as if it's tiring to be dead.
I ask her, *Are you weary?* and she says, *No,
are you? Yes,* I say and move into her arms
for a minute only, then she says she must

be off, something pressing, like the weight
on my heart as I wake, alive now, but her body
with me still, and warm, in the silk stockings
without shoes they dressed her in for burying.

THE THING YOU MUST REMEMBER

The thing you must remember is how, as a child,
you worked hours in the art room, the teacher's
hands over yours, molding the little clay dog.
You must remember how nothing mattered
but the imagined dog's fur, the shape of his ears
and his paws. The gray clay felt dangerous,
your small hands were pressing what you couldn't
say with your limited words. When the dog's back
stiffened, then cracked to white shards
in the kiln, you learned how the beautiful
suffers from too much attention, how clumsy
a single vision can grow, and fragile
with trying too hard. The thing you must
remember is the art teacher's capable
hands: large, rough and grainy,
over yours, holding on.

FAR

In this photograph it is Whitby, Yorkshire,
but it could be anywhere there's ocean
and nothing breathing. There's only
a road here, a slight incline, no people.
The sky is damasked with whites
that could be clouds, or scarf threads
or the photographer's cataracts.
The severe symmetry of the sea wall is also
a soft working of mortar, stone and sand.
The neat road lines were painted here
on a hot day by someone with a family
and who knows what he was thinking?
                        Anything can happen.
Perhaps a child will walk this road one day
and open and close a green umbrella against the sun.
Or an old man may walk here for exercise
and, thinking of something he did
or something he once ate, touch his wrist
delicately, as a dancer might. Anything.
                        Years from now
there may be a sick cat on this road howling
and hugging to the sea wall so as
not to have to look at the terrible water,
inventing from her pain whatever's missing,
blankets, or baskets, or affectionate arms.
As, I provide now the full singing weather,
the remembered talk of friends who have died,
far from where you had to stand
to get this shot so empty.

A SMALL PAUSE SURROUNDED
BY THE WEATHER

I'm out early in the morning, walking
with my old dog who thinks she is a pup
today because the weather's good.
She runs through fields of chicory
and ironweed, bobbing up and down
between blue and purple flowers.
She's forgotten she is old
and has arthritis and, right now,
I do not want to call her back.
I love how she is ignorant of ailments
and of death. She runs because the air
is clear and sharp today, because
the sun is warm and dappled through
the trees. The vernacular of dog
is only present. Time is just a small
pause surrounded by the weather.
Maybe later she will hurt and I will
build a fire for her to lie beside
on her green rug. For now
she stretches all her cells as far
as they will go through the fields
in the warm morning sun.

BEFORE WINTER

Sometimes inside us
like a forest at dusk
there are trees that move in the wind.

Or, as inside a house,
there may be only a view of trees
from an attic window
the orange leaves and black limbs
barely breathing as cars pass beneath.
They are framed by the white wood house next door
and streaked with gray sky.

The view is through a small green pane,
the curtains pushed back,
where sometimes a woman stands
and notices the morning scent
her son's shoulder left on her palms.

Sometimes inside us
a swirl of white wind starts up
among all that remains of October:
leaves fallen and pasted to wet streets,
the bare branches split by heavy rain.

We stay as still as the roots
of the trees we imagine holding
in solid earth, as rich
and black as perpendicular lines.

We are held steady by the roof of the attic,
the familiar cracks under the eaves.
We reach out for the dark walls
and banisters, each other's hands.

HEART FIRE

Three months since your young son shot himself
and, of course, no one knows why. It was October.
Maybe he was following the smell of dying leaves
or the warmth of the fire in the heart, so hard
to locate in a country always readying for war.

One afternoon we sat together on your floor, drinking
tea and listening to Brahms on the radio. He would
have liked this music, you told me. He would have liked
everything I like now and what he wouldn't like I don't
like either. He has made the whole world look like him.

Today, driving into Pittsburgh, I see you are right.
The sky is cold blue like a shirt I once saw him
wear and the bare trees are dark, like his hair.
I see how vulnerable the grasses are, pale and flimsy
by the roadsides, trying to stand straight in the wind.

At Canonsburg, all the pink and green and purple houses
have the same slant of roof toward the hill, like toys
because I'm thinking about children, how sometimes
we want to give them up if they seem odd and distant,
yet even if they die before us, we cannot let them go.

I see your son in landscapes as I drive, in a twist
of light behind a barn before the suburbs start,
or under a suburban street light where a tall boy
with a basketball has limbs like those he had just
outgrown. Because I want to think he's not alone,

I invent for him a heart fire even the unenlightened
living are sometimes allowed to see. It burns past
the white fluorescence of the city, past the steel mills
working off and on as they tell us we need, or don't
need, heavy industry for fuel, or war. Your son

keeps me company, driving down the last hill into
Pittsburgh, in the tunnel as I push for good position
in the lanes. He is with me as I spot the shiny cables
of the bridge and gear down, as all the lights beyond
the river come on now, across his safe, perfected face.

ANYTHING WE LEAVE FOREVER

The hills stand in each other's shadows at dusk
and I stare off at them, stunned, the way I'd be
if, walking through a strange town one day,
I looked down and found all the smooth stones
I piled up so carefully and then abandoned
as a child. I want to say it's the contrast
that startles me: black limbs against flat sun.
It's not that, but how the day remains behind
the purple rim of light; how anything we leave
forever, in the grand way, returns to us
unsummoned and at last without remorse, in details
like the tracery of twigs here in this evening
light behind the trees. Five miles across the valley,
the gold reliquaries of the afternoon are stored:
spiny branches cupped by clouds, the finger bones
of saints clicking in the satchels of the sky.

CIVILIZATION

"Weeds already hid the ashes, and wild flowers were in bloom among the city's bones. The bomb had not only left the underground organs of the plants intact; it had stimulated them. Everywhere were bluets and Spanish bayonets, goosefoot, morning glories and day lilies, the hairy-fruited bean, purslane and clotbur and sesame and panic grass and fever-few."
      —John Hersey, *Hiroshima*

Back from the West I chop aubergines for ratatouille
and think about Fort Laramie, Wyoming, how the military
is supposed to civilize, so they sent soldiers in uniform
with guns out to the plains to protect the authority
of table napkins, silverware, and what they wanted
for their property. The military does, of course,
convince, as the white fruit of eggplant is convinced
to a dusky brown as soon as it hits the hostile air.

The purple skins now strewn across my countertop
look like episcopal robes, shirred and broken down.
Religion civilizes too, I guess, and music, in the slow
passion that underrides a fugue but always seems to check
whatever wants to run amuck in violins. Fugal form
presumes a lot to flee from and it takes a long time
to develop a subtle sauce with more than three herbs.
The further east you come, the older the burying

grounds, until at last in Massachusetts, you can trace
back three centuries of patriot Websters and Felts
on the granite stones. I can't remember my catechism,
if I put the parsley in this sauce, or where my own
grandfather is buried. Outside my window the birds
make dark cacophony together, preparing their removal
South in organized bands. They sound like feral children
caught in branches, or the reckless weapons I never

63

want to think of. But they're in my mind all the time now,
persistent as the crickets are, kicking up their ruckus
by the narrow quiet streets, tame enough, and populous
among deciduous trees. It's fall and birds are leaving,
the red leaves are drifting down again. In the East
the wind blows too, but stops from time to time, as
it does not on Nebraska prairie where, not so long ago,
the pioneer women took up housekeeping in sod houses,

five feet of dirt floor and a snake draped from the roof.
I like to think there's hope in history, the diligent
rebuilding after war, the enthusiasm of overland migration,
all barn raisings and quilting bees. But it takes so
long to generate a good antiquity, to fill a burying
ground, or to learn how to pray somebody home. Things
get lost along the way or fall apart in the wind.
Mobs take off in righteous indignation, or in a frenzy

of invention, like the fire we've made conspicuous,
and useless in the face of any etiquette we'd like
to think is civilized: theology or property law,
counterpoint, or my good dinner simmering on the stove.
East or west or south where birds go, what we know
is not enough. We must practice grim decorum, study
how to make, if there is time, a thousand paper
cranes to hold up against the last enlightenment.

NOTES

"As Close" is dedicated to Paula Clendenin.

The five poems on pages 19–23 are based on photographs by Walker Evans which are reproduced in *Walker Evans: Photographs from the Farm Security Administration, 1935–38* (New York, 1973). With the exception of "Among Elms and Maples, Morgantown, West Virginia, August, 1935," all of my poem titles are the same as Evans's titles for his photographs.

The historical information in "The Artist" is based on the accounts of the Donner party in Virginia Reed Murphy's *Across the Plains in the Donner Party: A Personal Narrative of the Overland Trip to California, 1846–47* (Colorado, 1980) and Bernard De Voto's *The Year of Decision: 1846* (Boston, 1943). The direct quotation from Patty Reed in my poem is attributed to her by De Voto.

"Sweet Resin" is dedicated to Jane Cooper.

"Far" is dedicated to Elizabeth Matheson.

"Before Winter" is dedicated to Sharon Goodman.

"Heart Fire" is in memory of Aaron Goodman (1962–1983).

PITT POETRY SERIES

Ed Ochester, General Editor

Archibald MacLeish, *The Great American Fourth of July Parade*
Peter Meinke, *Night Watch on the Chesapeake*
Peter Meinke, *Trying to Surprise God*
Judith Minty, *In the Presence of Mothers*
Carol Muske, *Wyndmere*
Leonard Nathan, *Carrying On: New & Selected Poems*
Leonard Nathan, *Holding Patterns*
Kathleen Norris, *The Middle of the World*
Sharon Olds, *Satan Says*
Alicia Ostriker, *The Imaginary Lover*
Greg Pape, *Border Crossings*
James Reiss, *Express*
David Rivard, *Torque*
William Pitt Root, *Faultdancing*
Liz Rosenberg, *The Fire Music*
Richard Shelton, *Selected Poems, 1969-1981*
Peggy Shumaker, *The Circle of Totems*
Arthur Smith, *Elegy on Independence Day*
Gary Soto, *Black Hair*
Gary Soto, *The Elements of San Joaquin*
Gary Soto, *The Tale of Sunlight*
Gary Soto, *Where Sparrows Work Hard*
Tomas Tranströmer, *Windows & Stones: Selected Poems*
Chase Twichell, *Northern Spy*
Chase Twichell, *The Odds*
Leslie Ullman, *Dreams by No One's Daughter*
Constance Urdang, *Only the World*
Ronald Wallace, *People and Dog in the Sun*
Ronald Wallace, *Tunes for Bears to Dance To*
Cary Waterman, *The Salamander Migration and Other Poems*
Bruce Weigl, *A Romance*
Robley Wilson, Jr., *Kingdoms of the Ordinary*
David Wojahn, *Glassworks*
Paul Zimmer, *Family Reunion: Selected and New Poems*